City Kids

Poems by Patricia Hubbell • Illustrated by Teresa Flavin

MARSHALL CAVENDISH   NEW YORK

For city kids everywhere — P. H.

To Veronica — T. F.

Text copyright © 2001 by Patricia Hubbell
Illustrations copyright © 2001 by Teresa Flavin
All rights reserved.
Marshall Cavendish, 99 White Plains Road, Tarrytown, NY 10591

Library of Congress Cataloging-in-Publication data
Hubbell, Patricia.
City Kids : poems / Patricia Hubbell ; illustrated by Teresa Flavin.
    p.   cm.
ISBN 0-7614-5079-3
1. City and town life—Juvenile poetry. 2. Children's poetry, American.
[1. City and town life—Poetry. 2. American poetry.] I. Flavin, Teresa, ill. II. Title
PS3558 U22 C5   2001   811'.54—dc21   00-031528

The text of this book is set in 14 point Zapf Book Light.
The illustrations are rendered in watercolor and colored pencils.
Printed in Italy
6   5   4   3   2   1

Contents

The Doing Days

The doing days have started.
School is done, *done*, DONE!

Wonder what *I'll* be doing
Now summertime's begun?

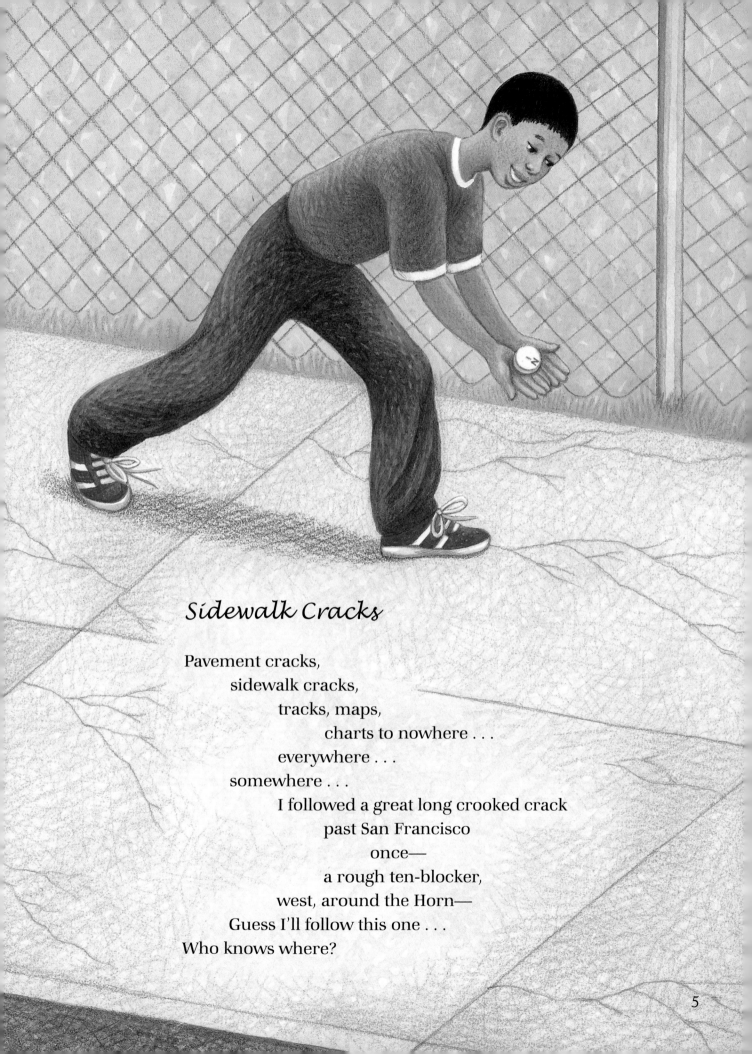

Sidewalk Cracks

Pavement cracks,
    sidewalk cracks,
        tracks, maps,
            charts to nowhere . . .
      everywhere . . .
somewhere . . .
        I followed a great long crooked crack
           past San Francisco
                once—
        a rough ten-blocker,
    west, around the Horn—
Guess I'll follow this one . . .
Who knows where?

City Kid

legs legs legs legs legs legs
legs legs legs legs legs legs
legs legs legs legs legs legs
legs legs legs legs legs legs
legs legs • ME • legs legs
legs legs legs legs legs legs
legs legs legs legs legs legs
legs legs legs legs legs legs
legs legs legs legs legs legs

Sneakers

On basketball courts
Everybody's old sneakers
Sing brand-new songs!

City Garden

See
Mr. McGregor's
Balcony?

He's got
Lettuce,
Tomatoes,
Beans—

Everything
But Peter
Rabbit!

8

Mugged

Cold hard stone
Under my seat—
Sylvia's grandma,
Mugged!

That old lady
Good as good
Mugged
In her own
Neighborhood.

Turn

Vials,
Needles,
Beneath my feet,
Broken glass
Littering my street.

I turn, turn, turn my back,
See the green grass growing
In the sidewalk crack.

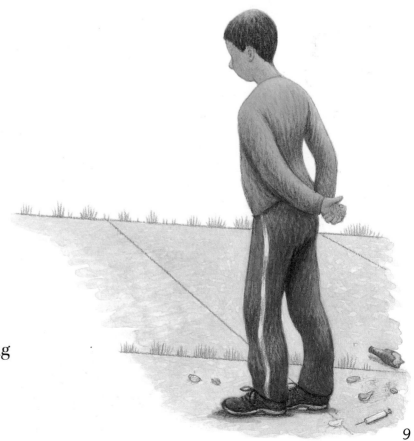

9

Fire Hydrant

Rusted at the mouth,
This old broken hydrant still
Gushes cold happiness!

Summer Afternoon

Fire hydrant's open!
Cops drove by and laughed!
Guess they wish
That they could feel
Fire hydrant *splash!*

11

Stickball

Pop says he played stickball
Just like me—
Chalking up the bases,
Dodging cars, trucks,
Hoping for the big win.

Tree Climbing

Up in
This tree,
My arms
Spread wide,

My heart's
So big,
It won't
Fit inside!

Stop!

Each time
I climb
Up in
A tree
Some cop
Yells,
    "STOP!"
And
Down
I
Drop.

(But then,
I do it
Again.)

Skateboard Lament

My skateboard's
got one
roller bent,
and I am feeling
discontent.

But Mama says,
"You hear *me* fuss?
That skateboard limps
just like my bus!"

City Mystery

My name—in the graffiti!
Who could have put it there?

Double Dutch

Double Dutch!
Double Dutch!

We're jumping to the rhythm
Of Double Dutch

Twirl! Whirl!
Leap! Skip!

Lift up, feet,
Don't trip

Twist, wrist!
Swing it faster,

First me,
Then my sister

Don't miss . . .
Don't miss . . .

Slow it down and then J*U*M*P OUT!

At the Pet Shop

I stopped at the pet shop,
Pressed my nose up to the glass—
Saw a bunch of wiggles
Behind that dirty glass—
Wiggle, puppies, wiggle,
Wiggle yourselves free!
Wiggle through that dirty glass,
Come on home with me!

18

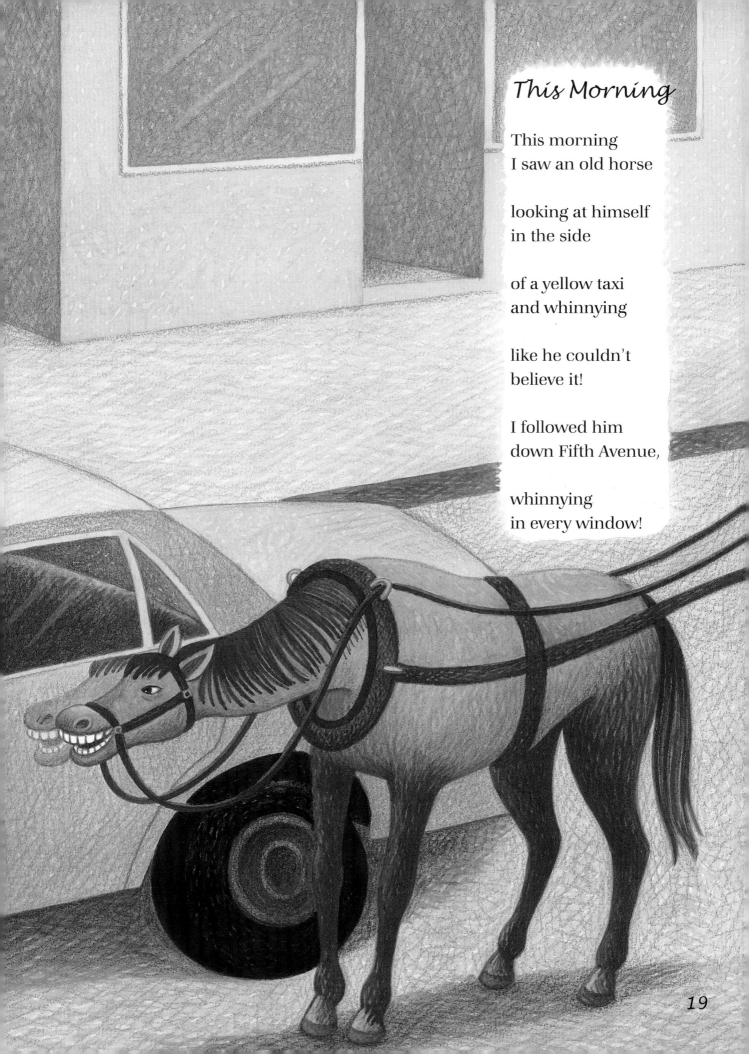

This Morning

This morning
I saw an old horse

looking at himself
in the side

of a yellow taxi
and whinnying

like he couldn't
believe it!

I followed him
down Fifth Avenue,

whinnying
in every window!

19

Gone

My friend
has gone away.
He didn't tell me why—

The smallest things
on earth today?
The shadow of this ant, and

me.

Bug Stop

One fuzzy caterpillar,
　Two green beetles
　　And about a thousand fiery ants
　　　All scrunched up in this sidewalk crack—
Must be a bus stop for bugs!

Change of Mind

Yesterday,
I rode my bike
To a far-away neighborhood—
And then—
   Pedaled home fast!

Changes

Yesterday,
   pigeons pecking
      under that big old tree—
        Today—
           only woodchips!

Baglady

Baglady sleeping—
Sparrow pecking at her packages—
"Scratching up a few old dreams," says Mama.

Skyscrapers

These
gray
walls
▭
▭
▭
go
up
and
up
and
up
and
up
forever
▭
▭
▭
reaching
for
the
sky
▭
▭
▭
like
Me

24

City Rainbow

A rainbow!
Hugging *my* building!

Guess I'll climb up
And s
        l
          i
           d
            e
              d
                o
                w
                n
                  to a brand-new land.

Closing Time

At night,
Steel gratings
Clang in place.
Every store
Wears metal lace.

Cold lace
To mark
The end of day—

Burglar, burglar, stay away!

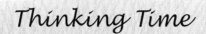
Thinking Time

Our television's broken,
There's silence in the air,
Silence in the living room,
Silence everywhere.

It gives my brain a time to think,
My eyes a time to see—
I love this silent evening time,
Just family and me.

City Full of Joy

Teacher asked us
What we dreamed—
I almost didn't say—
I almost didn't dare to tell
  My dream that day—

I dreamed about a city,
Beautiful and strong,
I dreamed about that city
  All night long—

I dreamed of flowers in the streets.
No guns. Safe place to play.
Dreamed that I was going there
  That same day—

Dreamed that everyone in town,
Every girl and boy,
Was dreaming the same dream as me
  —City full of joy!

28

Winter Morning

Car tracks
like white snakes

  slithering
    sliding

shedding their skins
  all over the city

and everybody

    hiding!

City Snow

Hustle!
Bustle!
Jostle!
Push!

Scurry!
Swarm!
Surge!
Rush!

And now,
    Quiet early morning snow . . .

First Week of December

Trees like forests everywhere,
The sidewalk's smelling fine.
A big sign says it's "Balsam,"
Wish that tallest tree were mine!

Secrets for the Wind

Look!
The playground swings
Are dancing in the snow—
And nobody in them!

I run and run,
Telling my secrets
To the wind.